Selected Poems of Padraic Colum

Padraic Colum, about age twenty. Courtesy of the
Padraic Colum Collection, Glen G. Bartle Library, State
University of New York at Binghamton.

Selected Poems of
PADRAIC COLUM

Edited by

SANFORD STERNLICHT

SYRACUSE UNIVERSITY PRESS

Permission to publish the poetry of Padraic Colum granted by the Estate of
Padraic Colum and Dolmen Press.

First Edition
First published 1989
99 98 97 96 95 94 93 92 91 90 89   6 5 4 3 2 1

The paper used in this publication meets the minimum requirements of American
National Standard for Information Sciences—Permanence of Paper for Printed
Library Materials, ANSI Z39.48-1984. ∞ ™

SANFORD STERNLICHT is a poet, critic, historian, and theater director. His books
include *Gull's Way* (poetry, 1961); *Love in Pompeii* (poetry, 1967); *John Webster's
Imagery and the Webster Canon* (1972); *John Masefield* (1977); *C. S. Forester* (1981);
Padraic Colum (1985); *Selected Short Stories of Padraic Colum* (Syracuse University
Press, 1985); *Selected Plays of Padraic Colum* (Syracuse University Press, 1986);
John Galsworthy (1987); and *R. F. Delderfield* (1988). He is also the author of
four books on American naval history, of which *McKinley's Bulldog: The Battle-
ship Oregon* (1977) was a Military Book Club and *Saturday Evening Post* Book
Club selection. Sanford Sternlicht is an adjunct professor of English at Syracuse
University.

Library of Congress Cataloging-in-Publication Data

Colum, Padraic, 1881–1972
      [Poems. Selections]
      Selected poems of Padraic colum / edited by Sanford Sternlicht.—
      1st ed.
            p.   cm.—(Irish studies)
      Bibliography: p.
      ISBN 0-8156-2458-1 (alk. paper)
      I. Sternlicht, Sanford V.   II. Title.   III. Series: Irish studies
(Syracuse, N.Y.)
PR6005.038A6   1989   88-21962
821'.912—dc19   CIP

CONTENTS

INTRODUCTION

SANFORD STERNLICHT

In 1927 AE dedicated his new book of verse, *Voices of the Stones*, to a middle-aged poet who had once been his protégé: Padraic Colum. In the dedicatory epistle he wrote:

> I made these voices in a rocky land,
> And I have named them Voices of the Stones,
> Although they do not keep that innocence
> Was shed on me when quiet made me kin
> To the cold immobile herd.
> All things have changed.

AE had remained in the "rocky land" while Colum had emigrated to America, but he lived in Dublin and not in the countryside, and thus he states that he had lost the innocence that derives from quiet contemplation of cattle. With great insight AE implies that Colum had not lost that innocence, and he was right, for although Colum lived most of his adult life in New York City, he remained a lyric, romantic, Irish poet whose work was rooted in the soil of Ireland that had nourished his ancestors and himself.

Richard Fallis says: "AE's greatest service to Irish literature . . . came . . . in his unceasing kindness to young writers . . . . Among his discoveries were James Joyce, Padraic Colum, James Stephens, Frank O'Connor."[1] In 1904 AE sponsored *New Songs*, a collection of poems by young Irish poets with fresh voices and refulgent vitality, who rejected the sentimental subjects and Swinburnean rhythms of the Celtic Twilight in order to articulate the lives, the work, the dreams, and the songs of the peasants and artisans of the rural nation as filtered through the personal experiences of the writers. The four Colum poems in *New Songs*, "The Plougher," "The Bells," "A Drover," and "A Poor Scholar," confirmed AE's belief that Colum, at age twenty-three, would make a significant contribution to Irish letters.

Furthermore, AE the mystic convinced Colum that he had a mission as a poet: to portray the fundamental nature of the Irish peasant experience as he had seen it and as he knew it, through what the younger poet called "the common furniture" of Irish daily life. As the years went by, Padraic Colum, playwright, storyteller, and folklorist as well as poet, created a special persona for himself: the Irish peasant bard, even when his haunts were New York, Dublin, London, Paris, and even the Riviera. He spent a lifetime growing into the role, cultivating and maintaining the look, manner, accent, joviality, sadness, flirtatiousness, and gentle, earthy wisdom of a nineteenth-century Irish village poet, while he produced a substantial body of fine lyric poetry that is a part of the Irish inheritance. In essence that is the sum of his contribution. In the end, as Zack Bowen notes, he was "content to be called poet."[2]

Padraic Colum lived ninety years. For forty-five of these years he was happily married to an intelligent, talented woman, the noted critic Mary Maguire Colum, who had been a remarkable beauty in her youth. A graduate of University College, Dublin, a suffragist, a teacher at Padraic Pearse's St. Enda's School, she was the ideal companion for the easy-going, minimally educated writer from Columbkille, County Longford. The Colums wrote, lectured, taught, and traveled together. Along with Thomas MacDonagh, James Stephens, and David Houston, they helped found the influential periodical *The Irish Review* (1911–1913).

When they grew gray and round and old, they came to be revered as the last survivors of a golden age and a shining place, the Dublin of the Literary Revival, for their friends and colleagues had been William Butler Yeats, James Joyce, John Millington Synge, Lady Gregory, the other founders of the Irish National Theatre Society, and the revolutionaries, statesmen, and politicians who created the Irish Republic, including Roger Casement, Padraic Pearse, Michael Collins, Arthur Griffith, and Eamon de Valera.

Colum was born on 8 December 1881, the first of eight children of Patrick Collumb, last of a long line of peasant farmers, but a graduate of the National School and a teacher in, and later master of, the Longford workhouse; and Susan MacCormack Collumb, the daughter of a gardener. Padraic loved to tell people he was born in a workhouse for the poor and he was, but not because his parents were indigent of course. He was named after his father and did not begin to call himself Padraic until 1901, when he joined the Gaelic League and the Irish Republican Army.

The senior Collumb, alas, had a great thirst, and he found his salary inadequate so he sailed for America to try his fortune in the New World. The family went to live with Susan's mother in County Cavan. Patrick failed, limped home, and took a position as clerk in the Sandy Cove Railway Station near Dublin. He became stationmaster and obtained a job for his eldest as a railway delivery boy. Colum had received only eight years of formal education when at age seventeen he passed an examination for a clerkship in the Irish Railway Clearing House on Kildare Street in Dublin. After a nine-hour workday (six per week) Colum would write his poetry and plays. Soon he was patronized by Arthur Griffith, the publisher, and Sinn Fein, leader and later first president of free Ireland, and he began to drill with the secret and illegal Irish Republican Army.

In 1902 Griffith started to publish Colum's nationalistic verse in the *United Irishman*, fiery pieces Colum later said were well lost. He also published short plays by Colum, one of which, "The Saxon Shillin'," won a three guineas' prize for a play that would help discourage young Irishmen from enlisting in the British army. As a result Colum was invited by Frank Fay and his brother Willie (W. G. Fay) to join the newly formed Irish National Dramatic Company as both playwright and actor. Soon, the company joined with the Irish Literary Theatre, founded in 1899 by Yeats, Lady Gregory, George Moore, and Edward Martyn. In the opening program Maud Gonne performed the title role in *Kathleen ni Houlihan*, and Padraic Colum appeared in *Deirdre* as Buinne, son of Fergus. The combined company was a great success. Its new name was the Irish National Theatre Society and then the Irish National Theatre Company. AE was elected first president but modestly declined in favor of Yeats. A visionary national theater had been established that in a short time would lead to the creation of the immortal Abbey Theatre Company.

Colum's first full-length play was *Broken Soil*, later rewritten as *The Fiddler's House*; but it was his second play, *The Land*, which opened in the newly-acquired Abbey Theatre on 9 June 1905, that gave the theater its initial success. With *The Land* Colum created a genre, the peasant play, that would hold the boards for over forty years.

Alas, the headstrong young man quarreled with Yeats and the Fays and quit the Irish National Theatre Company. Lady Gregory tried to get him to return, but he refused. The Abbey would perform Colum's last successful commercial play, *Thomas Muskerry*, in 1910; but essentially, Colum's professional career as a play-wright was over, although for the rest of his life he continued to write, rewrite, and strive for production of his plays.

Meanwhile, Colum's first book of poetry, *Wild Earth*, had been published in 1907 and had been well received. The poems in *Wild Earth* are the foundation of Colum's poetic canon. He seldom would deviate from, or improve on the clarity, the basic simplicity, the strength, the vitality, and the excellent lyrical quality of some of these verses, such as "A Connachtman," and "Dermott Donn MacMorna." The collection is not merely about peasant life, the ploughers and the drovers, and the young girls without men. Rather, it primarily depicts the nobility of the men and women who lived in the ancient ways, close to the sky and the soil, and who were inherently endowed with the elemental understanding of life and death and the eternal cycle of the seasons.

With the success of *Wild Earth* and after the break with the Abbey, Colum began to devote most of his creative energies to verse; and when an American philanthropist, Thomas Hughes Kelly, gave Colum an annuity to pursue his writing, the poet-playwright was able to devote his life to his craft. In 1909 he met his Molly with her cloud of red-gold hair and they were married three years later. But then the Kelly funds ran out, and although the Colums loved the heady artistic and political milieu of pre-Rebellion Dublin, enjoying their friendships with many of Ireland's finest writers and artists, they could not survive financially on the income from free-lance writing. Therefore, in 1914, they decided to make a trip to America. One of Colum's aunts, who lived in Pittsburgh, had offered to fund a visit for the newlyweds. The Colums intended only to look things over and most likely return to Dublin; but the outbreak of World War I prevented that, and after a brief sojourn in Pittsburgh, the couple moved to New York City, where Colum continued to write poetry. He worked for the cause of Irish independence by lecturing, writing, and fund raising for Eamon de Valera. Furthermore, he began a secondary but more lucrative literary career as a successful writer of books for young people. It was the latter that provided much of the Colum livelihood for most of his life in America.

In 1916 *Wild Earth and Other Poems* was published in New York. It immediately established Colum as an important voice of Irish exile, coming out as it did at the time of the Easter Rebellion. It also made Colum many influential friends on the American literary scene, including Carl Sandburg, Edgar Lee Masters, Sherwood Anderson, Vachel Lindsay, and Harriet Monroe, the founder of *Poetry* (Chicago). Later, the Colums would establish long-term relationships with Robert Frost, Edward Arlington Robinson, Van Wyck Brooks, Amy Lowell, Somerset Maugham, Ezra Pound, and Elinor Wylie. *Wild Earth and Other Poems* was revised and reissued in 1922, 1927, and 1950. Colum was a lifelong tinkerer with and "improver" of his poetry.

From the beginning Colum's poetry collections received favorable reviews, but there was seldom much critical follow-up. Neither obscure, solipsistic, nor gnomic, his verse seemed to frustrate critics. L. A. G. Strong puts his finger on the reason: "The work of Padraic Colum has had little critical attention, not through neglect or ignorance, but because its central quality is one with which literary criticism has little to do. Simplicity cannot be analyzed."[3]

In the spirited, affluent 1920s the Colums became part of the peripatetic international literary scene. There were visits to Dublin, to Paris to see the Joyces and to help James with his manuscripts as well as his publishing, family, and financial problems, and even to Hawaii, where Colum had been invited by the Hawaiian Legislature to survey and collect the folktales of the territory and prepare them for publication by Yale University Press. Three folklore volumes resulted: *The Gateway of the Day* (1924), *The Bright Island* (1925), and eventually *Legends of Hawaii* (1937), a one-volume combination of the first two books.

Meanwhile, Macmillan had published his next volume of verse, *Dramatic Legends and Other Poems* (1922), and his first novel, *Castle Conquer* (1923). Colum dedicated *Dramatic Legends* to Molly, of whom he lovingly says:

> Sweetheart and comrade, I gave you
> The waters' marches and the forest's bound,
> The valley-filling cloud, the trees that set
> The rains beneath their roots, out of this well.

In essence he offers her the world he creates in the poems that follow.

Dramatic Legends is only partially successful. The first sixteen short poems in the section called "Poems: Country Songs" are more forced and overtly contrived than Colum's earlier work. He is trying to maintain the Old Ireland connection, his stock in trade and his greatest asset as an exile poet, but it is slipping and fading at least for the time being. The second section of *Dramatic Legends* adds new animal poems, such as "The Bison," "The Hummingbird," and "The Monkeys," to the menagerie he had begun in *Wild Earth and Other Poems* with "River Mates," a poem about otters. Colum not only loved the little people of the world, he loved the humble and the gentle animals as well as the trees and the flowers.

Creatures (1927) expanded Colum's zoo with new poems about "Crows," "Plovers," "Asses," "Night Flyers," "Macaws," "Condors," and even "Aquarium Fish." *Old Pastures* (1930) introduced a group of flower poems and several moving and intense psychological studies of men and women in emotional extremis: grieving, caught in sexual passion, falling into unrequitable love, unable to communicate. These poems, particularly "At the Fore of the Year," "A Man Bereaved," "Branding the Foals," and "Scanderbeg," are among the best examples of a kind of Colum poetry in which, like a dramatic soliloquy, the poet presents a narration in which either the persona or the subject reveals him or herself, or is revealed, in a light antithetic to what the illuminated character intended or expected.

In *Poems* (1932) Colum collected and reordered most of the pieces that had appeared in *New Songs*, *Wild Earth*, the 1916 *Wild Earth*, *Dramatic Legends*, *Creatures*, and *Old Pastures*. He would radically reassemble his canon once more in *The Poet's Circuits* (1960), but *Poems* clearly indicates that except for the late poems of *Irish Elegies* (1958, 1961, 1966) and particularly *Images of Departure* (1969), Colum at fifty had written almost all of his memorable verse.

Concurrent with the publication of *Poems* the Great Depression hit the Colums hard. After sixteen years of collaboration Colum's publisher, Macmillan, decided to terminate their business relationship. Colum complained, blustered, unlimbered his Irish version of "chutzpah" probably learned from the outspoken Molly, threatened calumny in the writing community, and managed to get back on the payroll, although at a reduced salary. Of course, the trans-Atlanticing had to be cut back and the Riviera abandoned. Fortunately, Molly obtained an excellent job as an editor at the *Forum*, and they both received winter teaching appointments at the University of Miami. Later, they would also team teach at Columbia University, University of Wisconsin, and City

College of New York. With typical modesty Colum announced that he was not much of a teacher; Molly was the real teacher, but he could "stir up a bit of interest in poetry."[4]

Padraic Colum always thought of ancient Ireland in epic terms. He got that much at least from Yeats. He believed the Irish needed and deserved a great, popular epic poem like the *Iliad* or the *Aeneid*, and he tried to write it. *The Story of Lowry Maen* (1937) resulted. In 1,800 lines of blank verse, his longest poem, Colum tells a Bronze Age tale of an exiled young prince who, after years of trial, returns to his native Ireland at the head of a foreign army to claim his usurped throne. The nostalgic epic fails, however, for it is not memorable either in narrative line or language, and the resolution, without a great struggle, is disappointing, unsatisfying, and anticlimactic. The work falls into the crack opened by Colum's dilemma: he wanted the epic to be complex and mature, but at the same time he tried to make it nonviolent and thus suitable for young readers or for those who publish or buy books for the young. As a result *Lowry Maen* had no audience.

Flower Pieces (1938) is more successful. Colum is back doing what he did best: crafting short, exquisite, visually evocative lyrics. Seventeen tight poems, like Postimpressionist paintings, document Colum's childlike love of bright colors and the tiny beauties of life like "The Hollyhocks," "The Lilies," "The Tulips," and "The Roses."

It was fifteen years before another book of Colum's poetry appeared. During much of the intervening time Colum, besides writing books for young people, was working on what he hoped would be an epic historical, three-volume novel of nineteenth-century Ireland. The first and only completed volume came out in 1957 as *The Flying Swans*. An indifferent critical reception discouraged Colum. Simultaneously, he was struggling with the difficult and politically sensitive biography of his old friend Arthur Griffith, which would be published as *Ourselves Alone* (1959).

A biography of James Joyce was also in progress during this period. The Colums had said good-bye to the Joyces for the last time in 1939, just before the war began. Joyce had hustled his old friends out of Europe and safely back to America. He died in Zurich in January 1941. His wife, Nora, wrote to the Colums when the war ended. She was ill, destitute, distraught, and reduced to selling her husband's manuscripts. The Colums, far from affluent themselves, sent her money at once. They had always been good friends to the Joyces, generous with time, advice, personal aid, and, when possible, money. The final result of the long friendship was *Our Friend James Joyce* (1958), coauthored by Molly and Padraic. It is a charming, anecdotal work that, of all Joyce biographies, captures the human being in his several habitats most successfully.

In 1953 Colum published *The Collected Poems of Padraic Colum* but it is essentially a reprint of *Poems* (1932). Of the 109 pieces included, 98 are from *Poems*. "An Old Song Re-sung" and "Before the Fair" are the only outstanding additions to the canon. *Collected Poems* was well received. There was a whole new generation of critics to impress. Few if any compared the contents with *Poems*. The favorable reception proved to be an inspiration for Colum. He began to write and publish poetry again with a renewed vigor.

In *The Vegetable Kingdom* (1954) Colum incorporated all of *Flower Pieces*, plus flower poems from *Old Pastures* and *Poems*, and then filled out his verse garden with trees and vines and more flowers. He exults in his revived power of evocation. He adores "The Popular Tree" because it is a child of the Celtic land.

"Irises" stun him with their variegated beauty. "Dahlias" recall ancient Greece. Nothing is nugatory or without history. Eighteen new poems sparkle freshly in *The Vegetable Kingdom*, and in the last piece, "To Saint Fiacre, Patron of Gardens," an old gardener, like Colum himself, shapes order out of chaos and is the nurturer of civilization. No self-identification could have been more plausible for Colum, grandson of a professional gardener and lifelong cultivator of scores of brief lyrics about flora and fauna.

Molly died in 1957 while she and Padraic were working on *Our Friend James Joyce*. Very ill during her last year, she had contributed little to the book. Most of the work is his, but Padraic, always generous and gallant, had her name listed first. His loss was great. They had not only been wife and husband but best friends. Without children they relied upon each other for love and support. Fortunately for Colum, Molly's nephew, Emmet Greene, a writer and editor, came to live with him and, along with other friends, helped and encouraged Colum to travel, lecture, and write.

The uneven *Ten Poems* (1957) contains some weak verse but also one of Colum's finest later poems, "The Book of Kells," depicting the work of a medieval manuscript illuminator and based on the great treasure in Trinity College Library. Colum honors the illuminator, the visual creator of saints and ordinary people, plants and animals, the real and the mythological. The scribe, and by implication poets like Colum, works "in nomine Domini / Qui fecit caelum et terram."

In the final years of the 1950s, after he had reached his seventy-fifth birthday, and after Molly had passed away, Colum began to reminisce about the many important figures of Irish history and culture he had known, admired, respected, and cared for. They included poets, scholars, politicians, soldiers, revolutionaries, actors, businessmen, and clerics. They were all gone, and he alone remained to tell their story to the young. This process of review and revising judgments provoked a last blooming of poetic vitality in the old poet as Irish nationalism and patriotism surged anew. In a sense Colum's heart returned to Ireland a decade before his body did. He became a visitor to his memories. An old man, aware of short breath and time, walked with his young self in the changed land, and yet, because of memory, the unchanged paths and days of his youth.

In the drama the return manifested itself in the writing of five Noh Plays, *Moytura*, *Glendalough*, *Cloughoughter*, *Monasterboice*, and *Kilmore* (1961–1966), his finest dramatic efforts after the Abbey period. These Japanese-like plays, which are about Sir William Wilde, Charles Stuart Parnell, Roger Casement, James Joyce, and Henry Joy McCracken, not only reflect Colum's return to Irish historical and cultural themes, but they are also an unstated homage to Yeats, with whom Colum had quarreled so long ago, but who had introduced the Noh Play into Irish and, indeed, Western drama.

In poetry the new flowering was first manifested in *Irish Elegies*, first published in 1958, but added to in 1961 and 1963. Even though most of the poems had earlier versions, the Irish people and the critics embraced them as new born. Colum's long dead friends were now heroes in history books. Elegized are "The Rebel, Roger Casement," "The Scholar, Kuno Meyer," "The Painter, John Butler Yeats," "The Statesman, Arthur Griffith," "The Pilgrim, Thomas Hughes Kelly," "The Artificer, James Joyce," "The Player, Dudley Digges," "The Poet, Seumas O'Sullivan," and the "The Magister, Monsignor Pádraig de Brún."

Colum next took almost his entire canon and shuffled the poems into eight groups, which he called circuits, and brought out *The Poet's Circuits* (1960). The circuits are "The House," "Field and Road," "Things More Ancient," "The Glens," "The Town," "Women in the House," "People on the Road," and "Monuments." Essentially, the book is *Collected Poems* revisited. New in *The Poet's Circuits* are some of the forepieces and after-pieces he wrote to bracket the circuits. Most significant is the first forepiece, a long autobiographical narrative about youthful self-discovery, artistic maturation, and the mystery of creativity that echoes in form, content, and quality Wordsworth's *Prelude*. The forepiece, set about 1900, features sharp characterization of Irish rural types, a mentor figure based on Colum's uncle Mickey Burns, and a flood of exquisite literal imagery.

The Poet's Circuit was well received by yet another generation of critics and readers coming freshly to Colum's work, for seventeen years had passed between *Collected Poems* and the "new" anthology. Moreover, the younger critics and scholars realized that the "mir-acle" of Padraic Colum was that despite, or because of, a lifetime of self-imposed exile, turn-of-the-century Ireland never left Co-lum, in the same way that Joyce's Dublin of Bloomsday never deserted the novelist in his lifetime of exile.

The triumph of Colum's late "return" is his final collection of poetry, *Images of Departure* (1969). It is, in fact, an outstanding effort for a poet of any age, but when one considers that the twenty-five new poems in *Images* are the work of a writer in his mid-eighties, the achievement appears all the greater. The new work is simultaneously personal and universal. In the new poems he sadly but lovingly remembers his wife, as in "Expecting No One," and his mother in "After Speaking of One Who Died a Long Time Before." He says good-bye to the memory of friends, the walks of Old Dublin he loved, as in "In St. Stephen's Green," and he recalls the old and poor folk of his childhood days in

"Day's End." *Images of Departure* is a moving farewell to art and to life. In the final creative period of a long fruitful life, the poet himself steps to the center stage of his work. In a burst of romanticism the first person flourishes, recollected love and friendship live again in art, and death is faced with resignation and sadness, but also hope.

Colum died at the Parkway Pavilion in Enfield, Connecticut, on 11 January 1972, one month past his ninetieth birthday. The body was placed on view at the Abbey Funeral Home on Lexington Avenue and Sixty-seventh Street in Manhattan. St. Patrick's Cathedral conducted a high mass of the Resurrection, and Padraic Colum was taken home to Ireland for interment in Molly's grave on a hillside in St. Fintan Cemetery, Sutton, County Dublin. The gravesite overlooks beautiful Dublin Bay and the mouth of the River Liffey.

A younger poet, Padraic Fiacc, wrote: "Colum, after all, was a link to me, a young writer, with an Ireland that had so withered already it might never have existed . . . . About the man himself is always the boy who stood at the workhouse window and watched the wandering, rootless Ireland of the children of the great hunger."[5]

In his youth Colum selected three Irish models for his work as a poet, and his best efforts, those poems with Irish subject and substance, are the pieces that ring true to the values, techniques, and sensibilities he extracted from his literary antecedents, poets whom he believed could help him achieve his dream of becoming the National Poet of Ireland. Most obviously, there is the debt to Thomas Moore (1779–1852). In Moore's delicate, moving, sentimental lyrics Colum found a way to incorporate Irish linguistic patterns and pastoral subjects into his own lyricism. Colum's mother had shared her love for Moore's *Irish Melodies* (1808) with him. Colum greatly desired that his own poems, at least some of them, would be accepted into the canon of "anonymous" Irish folksongs as many of Moore's had. It came to pass. Some of Colum's lyrics are sung in the schools of Ireland today, and the children have no idea of their authorship. They are merely "old songs."

The poet and antiquarian Sir Samuel Ferguson (1810–1886) provided Colum with a model for his attempt to revivify in poetry the Heroic Age of Ireland. Ferguson's epic and folk verses in *Lays of the Western Gael* (1865) and *Congal* (1872) inspired and influenced a wide range of Colum's poetry from his epic *The Story of Lowry Maen* through a variety of pieces based on historical or folk subjects, such as "At Cashel," "The Ballad of Downal Baun," "The Deer of Ireland," "Egan O'Rahilly's Vision," "Ferns Castle," and "The Lament of Queen Gormlai."

Colum never let the reading public forget that he was different from Yeats, AE, Lady Gregory, and the other writers who came out of the Protestant ascendancy. He was a son of the Roman Catholic peasantry, and a descendant of the ancient Celtic people. He and his forebearers were the true inheritors of the heroic Irish tradition, the tradition Ferguson had shown him. Although they were Christian, the Irish peasantry retained a knowledge and appreciation of their pagan roots through mythology and folklore. Colum saw that it was his sacred duty to continue and to advance that vital, sustaining, and binding awareness. The men and women of the fields were the children of the old, disinherited nobility. The ancient legends were their patrimony. That they stoically endured their suffering so long, that they maintained their piety in the face of prejudice and persecution, that they remained dignified, charitable, and hospitable in the face of grinding poverty were all proof for Colum of their inherent gentility. Colum's ploughers, scythemen, ballad makers, knitters, drovers, honey sellers, old women, spadesmen, scribes, and poor scholars were the true aristocracy of Ireland, not the West Britons who lived in the great houses.

Thus a major contribution of Colum to the history of Irish literature is in his relationship to the poets of the Celtic Twilight. He adopted their interest in the legends of Heroic Ireland, stripped off the fascination for the occult, and diverted poetic energy and attention to the experience of common people of the countryside, the natural nobility. In this process he demanded "a curious inversion of traditional standards, so that what is menial, sentimental, even in rare instances vulgar is to be regarded as admirable and noble."[6] Yet unlike his mentors AE and Yeats he had no illusion about the second coming of the Heroic Age in any material sense.

Studying James Clarence Mangan (1803–1849), the inspirer of Yeats and Joyce too, showed Colum, in a more precise way than Moore, how to impose Gaelic syntax on an English vocabulary. Mangan's verse is based upon the popular syllabic or quantitative measure of Old and Medieval Irish verse instead of the accentual one of English verse. Colum, says Richard Loftus, "consistently attempts to achieve this kind of rhythm."[7] He places greater emphasis on sound patterns than most English language poets ordinarily would and considerably less emphasis on accentual metrics. The effect, when Colum is in his Irish mode, is a distinctly Gaelic one. When Colum is writing verse about the statue of General Phil Sheridan in Washington or trying to fabricate Hawaiian folk songs, or Arabic love poems, the language usually turns prosaic. In following Moore and Mangan, Colum, especially the younger Colum, exercises careful and precise control of meter and rhyme but seldom if ever at the expense of language, emotional value, and meaning. He enjoys the ballad stanza and the refrain line, and he turns extremely regular in his heavy use of the anapest, taking more freedom with the iambic foot. His metrics, combined with simple and direct language, support almost instant communication and can initially inspire song before thought. Ratiocination comes later for critic and reader. Subtleties appear with several subsequent readings and with the consideration of groups of lyrics. Furthermore, these subtleties arise not from dazzling conceits but from natural evocation and archetypal connection. Colum strives to make his reader feel at home in the poet's world and in the poet's vision, a world of acute sensory impression.

Many of Colum's finest poems, like "The Plougher," "A Poor Scholar of the Forties," and "An Old Woman of the Roads," are essentially dramatic monologues, a product of both his study of nineteenth-century poetry and, more significantly, his experience in the theater. In these kinds of poems a persona explicates the situation fate or Colum has placed him or her in, describes his or her life, and reacts to destiny. Moreover, the personae of Colum's monologues frequently indicate the character trait Colum most particularly admires: endurance. It is the source of their dignity; it is the secret of their survival.

In making my selections for this collection I have emphasized the poems on Irish subjects and themes. Colum is almost always at his poetic best when writing about the people and places of his childhood, youth, and early manhood. Hawaiian poems, pieces about "Carolina," Australia, or Mongolia simply do not ring true.

A problem to be faced resulted from Colum's continual rewriting. Both poems and plays were subject to sometimes lifelong revision. There are as many as five extant versions in print of a single poem. Generally, I have found that the earlier versions of poems are stronger. Extra lines accrued with time; spontaneity and freshness often atrophied; and beauty and precision occasionally were sacrificed for more discursiveness and "content." Therefore, most often I have selected the earlier, sometimes, slightly less-well-known version.

The order of this collection is generally chronological, as best I could discern from first publication, but sometimes Colum saved poems for years in order to have them for a specified kind of collection like *The Vegetable Kingdom* or *Irish Elegies*. Therefore, I have moved poems up in order when I have had evidence of composition earlier than indicated by first appearance in a collection. Chronological order is for most poets a developmental progression, and this is so for Colum. *Selected Poems* shows Colum's strong initial inspiration, his love of the people and land of Ireland, the nostalgia for the past, the growing sophistication, and the late but glorious renaissance of poetic vitality.

However, I begin *Selected Poems* with "Fore-Piece" from "Circuit One" of *The Poet's Circuits* because in the story of the relationship between the boy-poet persona and his mentor, Owen Paralon, is the account of Colum's coming to the calling of Irish bard. Paralon is modeled after Colum's uncle Mickey Burns, who with tales and fables and songs and snatches of history fired an imagination and created a poet.

Padraic Colum was a unique artist. He went his own way, writing poetry in the middle of the twentieth century much the way he had taught himself at the end of the nineteenth, and he did so without apology. He loved the life of the poet. He rejoiced in being an Irish poet. He remained true to his credo: "I have identified myself with a particular Irish memory, a particular Irish tradition; it is the memory and the tradition of the historic Irish people."[8]

NOTES

1. *The Irish Renaissance* (Syracuse, N.Y.: Syracuse University Press, 1977), p. 118.

2. *Padraic Colum: A Biographical Critical Introduction* (Carbondale, Ill.: Southern Illinois University Press, 1970), p. 58.

3. *Personal Remarks* (New York: Liveright, 1953), p. 79.

4. Letter in Padraic Colum Collection, S.U.N.Y. Binghamton.

5. "Remembering Padraic Colum," *Threshold* 37 (Winter 1986/87): 15.

6. Richard Loftus, *Nationalism in Modern Anglo-Irish Poetry* (Madison: University of Wisconsin Press, 1964), p. 184.

7. *Ibid.*, p. 178.

8. *The Road Round Ireland* (New York: Macmillan, 1926), p. vi.

POEMS

FORE-PIECE

I

From where the solitary crow, the grey,
Infamous in our sagas, fluttered over
The flatness of the bog, to where familiar
Crows gathered in the trees beside a house,
He drove me: there were miles of rutted road.

It was the Easter of my twentieth year,
And Easter was betokened: half-grown lambs
Beside their mothers in a rocky field;
Black cattle making tracks
Between the golden bushes of the whins;
The crops enclosed with hedges, and the bog
Rough with the heather that had shade of bloom.

As in Fenian stories
Some man unheard of forcefully comes in,
And by demands he makes turns things around
And changes someone's history, he came
Into my days that were unlike the heroes',
And his demand was only that I take
His hospitality. So here I was
Mounted beside him on his outside car
With mare between the shafts—Owen Paralon.

3

Not only in his advent was he like
The man in Fenian stories, but in the way
His speech became narration as we went
Between the hedgerows, for he told about
The fair of Ballinasloe, the three-day fair
Where one could prove oneself an Irishman
By quickness in the judgement of a horse.
It would be just as blundering, he averred,
For one like him to show misjudgement there,
As for one not to know the dance's figure
In house where people gathered on Shrove Night,
And had to place himself behind the door
For shame of ignorance; his story was of horses
Fed on choice oats and led around by owners,
And eyed by men who knew in lift of head
A horse's spirit, and his paces in
The way he lifted hooves upon the street.
And while he spoke of this, the big-boned mare
Went steadily and well.

                              Remembrance came to me:
My father's and my mother's forefathers
Lived where such fields
With crops and cattle brought the year around,
But we were born, myself and other children,
In borough where my father held an office,
And though the distance
To these old places were in tens of miles,
It meant for us, the children, ruggedness,
Strange faces and cramped houses, generations

One had not lived with, who instructed us
In other ways, whose kindness was from far.
And once when I had come to Confirmation,
And had received the seven ghostly gifts,
Among them being the Gift of Understanding,
I found myself in one of these thatched houses.
The only inmates, children welcomed me:
They made me one of that mysterious household
That children own; they even showed me
The footstep in the ash that was Saint Brighid's.

And now we came to where upon the trees
Crows with all harshness served discordant broods,
And here was my host's house, Owen Paralon's.
The walls were thick, as though some castle builder
Had stooped to raise a house that would have only
Bedrooms and attic over living room;
A farmer's house with grunting of the pigs,
And geese's gabble coming from the yard.
A comely woman stood upon the doorstep
To welcome me—the woman of the house.

The timber that the bog had long preserved
Blazed on the hearth; the benches, table,
Meal-chest and dresser, showed a craftsman's choice
Of oak or ash or elm, and fit design.
And there was that that gave largesse to all:
Above a wild duck with a glistening neck,
And brown dead hare, there shone a silver cup.

And who was I that with such great elation
Was brought into this house? One without mark,
And solitary, since I had been removed
From places I had known, one whose nearest
Were dead or scattered, one who had such thoughts
As those who have no prospects entertain—
Inconsequential, unfulfilling, void.
As profitless in friendship as in wage
My means of living; the solitariness
Was occupying mind, for I had found
A refuge in repository of books
Of dream and speculation, books that made
The world spectral for me, that I read
Fondly. Then this man came
And prayed that I would come to him some time,
And in the promise that I made to him
What challenge was there? I lived with reveries,
Soliloquies, and guesses that detained me,
And from these turning was to lose my way.
The promise that I gave went with resolve.

'A great man of his word', he said of me,
When we had eaten, and 'word' and 'man'
Took on a meaning over the hearthstone,
As though no one who had not pledged himself
Had title to be there. Johanna showed
That she already had good thought of me.

The pair were married half a lifetime; they
Had daughter only; she was gone from them,
And was a nun professed.

And why had he
Sought me and brought me to this seat beside
His hearth? Because as some day brings
A memory of a day when one had joy
And all things had a glow, he had bethought
Of one he met in some bright company
He was not used to, and that never again
He entered, or saw her ever again,
And then a memory had taken him,
And he had come to see one of her rearing,
(So chance was present in this happening!)
And having come, drew out of me a pledge.
(Yes, chance! But will had seconded the chance!)
And here was I who for this evening felt
A hostage in a land of golden whin,
Black cattle and the bog with heather rough.

He was a six-foot man, Owen Paralon,
But that good size
Was but a frame for him; his was a face
So clear of line a sculptor might have set it
Above the carved door of an oratory
With faces of the princes and the craftsmen
Whom he had known, faces that ne'er looked on
Olympian games nor consular processions,
But have proportion due to deed and thought.
The rugged brows
Above the deep-set eyes put him before
The easy-going; between brow and lip
The nose was straightly chiselled, and the mouth

Ready for speech, ready for judgements,
And there was humour in its changing line:
Indeed his face
Was like the land the light is quick upon
And changes from one instant to another.

Another evening when he sat with neighbours
To talk of farming matters, I was by
Where she, the woman of the house, used needle,
The wide spread of the quilt upon her knees,
The lamp, not candles, burning; there I heard
Talk of new grass and watched her fingers ply.

Night after night
The fire burned down in ashes, holding sparks
To be rekindled and to glow and fade
All through the day. I watched her draw the needle
Back to her shoulder, then put stitches through
The patch of red or black that she was quilting.
My gaze was held by these repeated motions.
And at the table Owen Paralon
And his three neighbours plotted grass in fields.

I sat where there was custom—
Where men were mindful of the coming grass,
And where upon her knees a quilt was growing
A homely grandeur, patched with red and black.
The bog-deal blazed:
I had no custom, and I lived at random:
I would go back to what was, would be mine—

Long walks at night about the streets of a town
Where no one knew me, and to musings over
Books that were musings of unplanted men.

   And now Owen Paralon and his three neighbours
Came to the hearth: the silver cup was brought him,
And whiskey for each man of us was poured
Out of a jar; we drank with ceremony:
An old-time leader had drunk out of it.

   'The quilt will be a cover for you, son,
When you come back,' Johanna said to me.
The pause she made, the needle at her shoulder
Was like a turn in verse. Then I saw more:
The red and black were made in tufted patches:
She raised the patch she would put needle through
With paper scraps were in a basket by her.
I lifted up
A scrap of paper, and saw lines upon it
Made by a quill, and saw they were in Latin,
And knew them Virgil's by their poetry
Although they were about the bulls and cows,
Their mating and the cleaning of their byres:
A Poor Scholar or a Hedge Schoolmaster
Copied from tattered book upon that page
For lads who sat here by the fireside
Generations gone: I took up other pages—
Old yellow broadsheets that were bluntly printed
And sung on streets of hangings and the like:
And there were some that were less public songs.

Another day and I was in a town
Whose buildings were a dingy Market-house,
And Court-house on the grand side. Crowd was there,
But 'Trial' was the muttered word I heard,
'Assize' I heard; there were no beasts
To give men reason for being on the street:
No bargaining. 'He bears a sentence, he.'
I turned round and saw sunken face,
And eyes that had no hope or light in them—
An old man with a desperate thing to say:
'He bears a sentence.' A young man went
Between the constables, the guards who showed
Some fear of sticks in men's hands or stones
Picked from the street. But there was pain for more
Than one arrest in face that there I looked on. . . .

Back in the days when I was still at school,
Street songs I heard and used the lines I heard
Running beside my hoop as children's rhymes,
Not knowing that the lines came out of conflict
That led to prison cells, demolished houses.
I came to know
The mounting tumult, banners and parades,
And torch-lit meetings, and the high debates
Were all to end a power that could take
Their fields from men who tilled them or who grazed,
The power to turn the cabins built of clay
Back into clay. I looked upon a grapple,
And what was hearsay now was spectacle.
'He bears a sentence!' Often and often
These words were said for many another man.

And then and there a band came into life
With rebel tune that lowered pompousness
Of Court-house and Assize, and made the going
Of one man towards the gaol gate memorable
As though the lines of a great pencil showed it.
And then another turn: red-coated men
On horses and with hounds, their heads held down,
Had come in and were passing by the crowd—
The owners of the countryside were they,
And they were riding with their hounds beside them
To where more mounted men stayed in a field.
Unruffledly they went; then from the field
A bugle rang out and another bugle
With domineering note, and then the hounds
Raised heads in eagerness; I looked towards the field
Where now the mounted men were gathering:
They made a patch of red beyond the town.

The patch of black I saw—Owen Paralon's—
The field he ploughed. —I saw him in the field
Where I went with the lad that brought his meal,
The ploughman's meal such as his father had,
And such as he had in these forty years:
Oat-cakes with butter that was laid as deep
As they were thick, and draughts of buttermilk.
Then watercress. I stepped up to the pool
And gathered leaves that gave the oaten cakes
A tang. When I stood up
The width of country was spread before me,
Coloured with blossom and the green of crop.
I heard the lark's song, and in the distance

11

Voices that were where household tasks were plied.
A heritage it was, and though some claimed it,
It was for those who could rejoice in it—
And who would come and, standing in this place,
Rejoice, and know that he or she rejoiced?

   The ploughman halted, left the plough at stand,
And walked his field as if he still had hold
Of the plough's handles; his head was high—

          Ere Beowulf's song
          Was from the ships,
          Ere Roland had set
          The horn to his lips.

          In Ogham strokes
          A name was writ,
          In his that name
          Is living yet.

          The strokes on the edge
          Of the stone might count
          The acres he owns
          On this bare mount.

          But he remembers
          The Ogham stone,
          And knows that he is
          Of the seed of Conn.

The nestling crows had come down on the grass,
And there were squawking, or were lifting up
Their wings. The time had come for me to leave.
Her litter raging, racing, pushing under
Her slack teats, and heading past
To gulp the mash, a sow was at the trough;
A gander stood
Urgent to have his geese get them away
Down to the cleanly pool. I looked into the yard.
All parting's grave because it leaves a doubt
If all has been fulfilled where one has been,
If all can be accomplished where one goes.
Johanna stood to take her leave of me
With a good prayer. Owen Paralon brought out
The big-boned mare, and yoked the outside car.
I mounted, and with Owen Paralon
Across from me, we took the road again
Between the hedgerows, and came to where
The long rails stretched out. 'I know that you will come
Back to us,' Owen Paralon said to me.
'Some time,' some time,' 'some time,' the puffing train.

II

Back in the town I turned into the harbour
That I had found: it was an old, dark house
Behind a hedge of variegated laurel,
And I would come to it after my hours
Of fruitless work, and mount the steps and enter
With hopes of great discoveries, and leave

13

With thoughts were like a rebels' company,
Unled, unbannered, with pikes for weapons.
I'd walk along an empty quayside then,
With thought emerging that I'd try to seize.

And that repository of the arcane,
The occult and prophetic: Huguenots,
Strangers in the land, becoming strangers
To their inheritance, had formed it,
But mainly one who owned the mansion: he
Had known fantastic Mathurin who wrote
Melmoth the Wanderer, and afterwards
Le Fanu, who told *House in the Churchyard*
And *Uncle Silas*, would come here and read
Of angels, apparitions, hauntings strange.
'Twas there I'd sit with a few other readers,
Old men who had the pride
That made them strive for erudition
Beyond what others have, some lonely knowledge
Reached by the fellows who leave commonsense
To others in the street, and so become
Prophets or pedants or the two in one.

I had been given entrance to the place
Because of service I had done the grandson
Of him who left the house and all was in it
To an illuminati fading always,
And with their remnant I would sit and read
Under the gaze of one portrayed in robes,
Banker-ambassador whose chairs we filled.

The century that held my twenty years
Came to an end, and as I walked the quayside
Alone, I felt within
Gropings for words and measure to give form
To what I'd read, the utterance that closed
The century before, in scene illumined
By the cold light was on the frozen seas,
'Farewell to you who die for kings of earth
Farewell, ye races without native land,
Farewell, ye lands without a people in them' —
Seraphita's cry in Balzac's story.
Some verses came to me as I turned homeward
Hearing the bell that marked the century's end.

I did not read much further in the books
Of that past century, or what I read
Gave me no leading, for in newspapers
There were reports of Owen Paralon:
How for a speech
Made in a market-place that had been cowed
By proclamation and assembly
Of armed men, he had been arrested,
And was now gaoled: there was a picture
Of his being hauled from seat of outside-car
By constables with desperate mien and grasp.

When the time came for me to get my leave
From office work, I left the town behind
And went to visit him, his term been served.

'You will come back to us,' he'd said to me,
And here was I where I'd departed from.
—You will come back to us. The one was here
Looked back upon a dream-bribed solitary
Who was not he.

        And then the outside-car
With big-boned mare between the shafts arrived,
And I was taken by the servant-boy
Between the hedgerows to Owen Paralon's,
And I was welcomed there with outstretched hands
And brought within.

  Seeing the bog-deal blaze upon the hearth,
The silver cup in place upon the shelf,
I thought things had not changed, and then I knew
Something was altered in Owen Paralon.
Though still his stature and his features were
Commanding, there was gauntness in his look:
Not as a man out of the Fenian stories,
With fullness of heroic energy,
Did he appear as he stood on the floor
Of his own house: it seemed as though the years
That had kept distance from him now flowed in,
So that a prime that had been barely reached
A little while before, was past for him.

  Our felon told us of the bed he slept on,
Too short for his full length, and of the 'skilly'
The prison porridge that was made so thin
There was no mouthful in it. As we sat
Beside the hearth with company around,

A neighbour said, 'All we went through in years
To win our land will be like stories told
Of wars and insurrections long ago.
Our children who will listen to such tales
Will see the Big House empty as the Castle.'
'Something is lost in every change that comes,'
Owen Paralon replied, 'and I can tell you
This house had once more life between its walls
Than it or house around will show again.'

Then he recalled: 'A carter mending harness
Was on that bench, and where the light was best
The thresher bound his flail with skin of eel.'
And then went on, 'A woman carding wool
Was there, a girl spinning yarn;
And there were others that the neighbours honoured,
Around the hearth—the poet and the scholar,
The pilgrim, and the story-teller, too.
And there a sack of leaves or heather-tops
For one who went the roads and had no bed—
The place was in the nook beside the hearth.
And there was she, the woman of the house
Attending all, and taking from the ovens
The high brown bread, baked from the wheat we cut
In bottom field, and ground in mill above us,
To serve as supper for the labourers,
With mug of milk beside the warm bread,
Butter, and goose egg there beside each platter.'
'A lively house indeed,' a neighbour said.
'I mind the songs, I mind the discourse in it.
But who'll have memory of them when we're gone?'

Then, later, when the neighbours had gone home,
And my housemates had left me for their bed,
I still kept place beside the covered fire.
I was alone.
Yet there were people with me, men and women
Who had abodes, who had a history,
And work, and humours, and the moiety
Of poetry tradition keeps in trust.
And I could hear,
The door being open, certain birds that flew
Between the clouds and bog, and I could hear
The cattle stirring in the byre, the horses,
Moving in their short sleeps, and while I stayed there
My mind took to itself a murmuring,
And there were words that it was fitted to,
Words that turned in furrows or in verses,
And took a shape, and went with certainty
Among surprises, and became a poem.

And the next day, when we went after sheep,
I told my poem to Owen Paralon,
And he made much of it and more of me.
' 'Tis long since we'd a poet hereabouts,'
He told me solemnly; and then he said,
'It is a day for me when I can show
A poet, one who comes beneath my roof.'
And then I knew
That I was given a place whose vacancy
Was oft disturbing. There was no commission
As for a magistrate, no ordination
As for a priest, but still tradition held

That every place that had a county name
Should own a poet, and on Owen Paralon's
Warrant, I was poet of the place.

From the one poem I made, another came,
And my investiture became my guidance—
(It was my drinking from the silver cup
Passed round the company in Owen Paralon's).
Then later, when my employment shifted,
And I was sent about the countryside
To register changes in the land's
Ownership, I went into the houses,
And on the by-ways, and to fairs and markets,
And followed roads unsettled men went on,
And took the part of poet.

Out of glimpses
Of days and nights of women and of men,
And often with the words they spoke to me,
Or verses they delivered, I made poems.
I did not neglect
To 'prove my poetry' as in by-gone days.
So in the springtime I would close a circuit,
And go between the hedgerows, when the whins
Were golden, and would come to where the crows
Fed their discordant broods, and go within
Owen Paralon's, and to a company
Whose minds words could enliven as the turf
Down-breaking made a kindling in the ash.
I told my poems, and as they say in stories,
The ford I found, they found the stepping-stones.

A POOR SCHOLAR OF THE FORTIES

My eyelids red and heavy are,
With bending o'er the smould'ring peat.
I know the Æneid now by heart,
My Virgil read in cold and heat.
In loneliness and hunger smart.
　　And I know Homer, too, I ween
　　As Munster poets know Oisin.

And I must walk this road that winds
'Twixt bog and bog, while east there lies
A city with its men and books,
With treasures open to the wise,
Heart-words from equals, comrade-looks;
　　Down here they have but tale and song,
　　They talk Repeal the whole night long.

"You teach Greek verbs and Latin nouns,"
The dreamer of young Ireland said.
"You do not hear the muffled call,
The sword being forged, the far-off tread
Of hosts to meet as Gael and Gall.
　　What good to us your wisdom store,
　　Your Latin verse, your Grecian lore?"

And what to me is Gael or Gall?
Less than the Latin or the Greek.

I teach these by the dim rush-light,
In smoky cabins night and week.
But what avail my teaching slight.
   Years hence in rustic speech, a phrase
   As in wild earth a Grecian vase!

THE PLOUGHER

Sunset and silence! A man: around him earth
    savage, earth broken;
Beside him two horses—a plough!

Earth savage, earth broken, the brutes, the dawn-
    man there in the sunset,
And the Plough that is twin to the Sword, that
    is founder of cities!

"Brute-tamer, plough-maker, earth-breaker!
    Can'st hear? There are ages between us.
"Is it praying you are as you stand there alone
    in the sunset?

"Surely our sky-born gods can be naught to you,
    earth child and earth master?
"Surely your thoughts are of Pan, or of Wotan,
    or of Dana?

"Yet, why give thought to the gods? Has Pan
    led your brutes where they stumble?
"Has Dana numbed pain of the child-bed, or Wotan
    put hands to your plough?

"What matter your foolish reply! O, man, stand-
    ing lone and bowed earthward,

"Your task is a day near its close. Give thanks
    to the night-giving God."

Slowly the darkness falls, the broken lands blend
    with the savage;
The brute-tamer stands by the brutes, a head's
    breadth only above them.

A head's breadth? Ay, but therein is hell's depth,
    and the height up to heaven,
And the thrones of the gods and their halls, their
    chariots, purples and splendours.

A DROVER

To Meath of the pastures,
From wet hills by the sea,
Through Leitrim and Longford
Go my cattle and me.

I hear in the darkness
Their slipping and breathing.
I name them the bye-ways
They're to pass without heeding.

Then the wet, winding roads,
Brown bogs with black water;
And my thoughts on white ships
And the King o' Spain's daughter.

O farmer, strong farmer!
You can spend at the fair
But your face you must turn
To your crops and your care.

And soldiers—red soldiers!
You've seen many lands;
But you walk two by two,
And by captain's commands.

O the smell of the beasts,
The wet wind in the morn;
And the proud and hard earth
Never broken for corn;

And the crowds at the fair,
The herds loosened and blind,
Loud words and dark faces
And the wild blood behind.

(O strong men with your best
I would strive breast to breast
I could quiet your herds
With my words, with my words.)

I will bring you, my kine,
Where there's grass to the knee;
But you'll think of scant croppings
Harsh with salt of the sea.

AN OLD WOMAN OF THE ROADS

O, to have a little house!
To own the hearth and stool and all!
The heaped up sods upon the fire
The pile of turf again' the wall!

To have a clock with weights and chains,
And pendulum swinging up and down!
A dresser filled with shining delph,
Speckled and white and blue and brown!

I could be busy all the day
Clearing and sweeping hearth and floor,
And fixing on their shelf again
My white and blue and speckled store!

I could be quiet there at night
Beside the fire and by myself,
Sure of a bed, and loth to leave
The ticking clock and shining delph!

THE SUILIER

I'm glad to lie on a sack of leaves
By a wasted fire and take my ease.
For the wind would strip me bare as a tree—
The wind would blow oul' age upon me.
And I'm dazed with the wind, the rain, and the cold.
    If I had only the good red gold
To buy me the comfort of a roof,
And under the thatch the brown of the smoke.
    I'd lie up in my painted room
Until my hired girl would come;
And when the sun had warmed my walls
I'd rise up in my silk and shawls,
And break my fast before the fire.
And I'd watch them that had to sweat
And shiver for shelter and what they ate.
The farmer digging in the fields,
The beggars going from gate to gate,
The horses striving with their loads,
And all the sights upon the roads.

I'd live my lone without clan nor care,
And none about me to crave a share.
The young have mocking, impudent ways,
And I'd never let them a-nigh my place.
And a child has often a pitiful face.
    I'd give the rambling fiddler rest,

And for me he would play his best.
And he'd have something to tell of me
From the Moat of Granard down to the sea!
And, though I'd keep distant, I'd let in
Oul' women who would card and spin
And clash with me, and I'd hear it said:
"Mor, who used to carry her head
As if she was a lady bred—
Has little enough in her house, they say—
And such-a-one's child I saw on the way
Scaring crows from a crop, and glad to get
In a warmer house, the bit to eat.
O, none are safe, and none secure,
And it's well for some whose bit is sure!"

I'd never grudge them the weight of their lands
If I had only the good, red gold
To huggle between my breast and my hands!

A CONNACHTMAN

It's my fear that my wake won't be quiet,
   Nor my wake-house a silent place:
For who would keep back the hundreds
   Who would touch my breast and face?

For the good men were ever my friends,
   From Galway back into Clare.
In strength, in sport, and in spending,
   I was foremost at the fair.

In music, in song, and in friendship,
   In contests by night and by day,
By all who knew it was given to me
   That I bore the branch away.

Now let Manus Joyce, my friend
   (If Manus be here in the place),
Make smooth the boards of the coffin
   That shortly will cover my face.

The old men will have their stories
   Of all the deeds in my days,
And the young men will stand by the coffin
   And be sure and clear in my praise.

But the girls will stay near the door,
    And they'll have but little to say:
They'll bend their heads, the young girls,
    And for a while they will pray.

And, going home in the dawning,
    They'll be quiet with the boys:
The girls will walk together,
    And seldom they'll lift the voice.

And then, between daybreak and dark,
    And between the hill and the sea,
Three Women come down from the Mountain
    Will raise the Keen over me.

But 'tis my grief that I will not hear,
    When the cuckoo cries in Glenart,
That the wind that lifts when the sails are loosed
    Will never lift my heart.

DERMOTT DONN MacMORNA

One day you'll come to my husband's door,
   Dermott Donn MacMorna,
One day you'll come to Hugh's dark door,
And the pain at my heart will be no more,
   Dermott Donn MacMorna!

From his bed, from his fire, I'll rise,
   Dermott Donn MacMorna,
From the bed of Hugh, from his fire I'll rise,
With my laugh for the pious, the quiet, the wise,
   Dermott Donn MacMorna!

Lonesome, lonesome, the house of Hugh;
   Dermott Donn MacMorna,
No cradle rocks in the house of Hugh;
The list'ning fire has thought of you,
   Dermott Donn MacMorna!

Out of this loneliness we will go,
   Dermott Donn MacMorna,
Together at last, we two will go
Down a darkening road with a gleam below.
Ah but the winds do bitter blow.
   Dermott Donn MacMorna!

A CRADLE SONG

O, men from the fields!
Come softly within.
Tread softly, softly,
O! men coming in.

Mavourneen is going
From me and from you,
To Mary, the Mother,
Whose mantle is blue!

From reek of the smoke
And cold of the floor,
And the peering of things
Across the half-door.

O, men from the fields!
Soft, softly come thro'.
Mary puts round him
Her mantle of blue.

ACROSS THE DOOR

The fiddles were playing and playing,
  The couples were out on the floor:
From converse and dancing he drew me,
  And across the door.

Ah! strange were the dim, wide meadows,
  And strange was the cloud-strewn sky,
And strange in the meadows the corncrakes,
  And they making cry!

The hawthorn bloom was by us.
  Around us the breath of the south.
White hawthorn, strange in the night-time—
  His kiss on my mouth!

A BALLAD MAKER

Once I loved a maiden fair,
  Over the hills and far away.
Lands she had and lovers to spare,
  Over the hills and far away.
And I was stooped and troubled sore,
And my face was pale, and the coat I wore
Was thin as my supper the night before.
  Over the hills and far away.

Once I passed in the Autumn late,
  Over the hills and far away.
Her bawn and byre and painted gate,
  Over the hills and far away.
She was leaning there in the twilight space
Sweet sorrow was on her fair young face,
And her wistful eyes were away from the place—
  Over the hills and far away.

Maybe she thought as she watched me come,
  Over the hills and far away;
With my awkward stride and my face so glum,
  Over the hills and far away.
"Spite of his stoop, he still is young;
They say he goes the Shee among,
Ballads he makes, I've heard them sung
  Over the hills and far away.

She gave me good-night in gentle wise,
  Over the hills and far away;
Shyly lifting to mine, dark eyes,
  Over the hills and far away.
What could I do but stop and speak,
And she no longer proud, but meek?
She plucked me a rose like her wild-rose cheek—
  Over the hills and far away.

To-morrow, Mavourneen a sleeveen weds,
  Over the hills and far away;
With corn in haggard and cattle in sheds,
  Over the hills and far away.
And I who have lost her—the dear, the rare—
Well, I got me this ballad to sing at the fair,
'Twill bring enough money to drown my care,
  Over the hills and far away.

THREE SPINNING SONGS

I

(A young girl sings:)

The Lannan Shee
Watched the young man Brian
Cross over the stile towards his father's door,
And she said, "No help,
For now he'll see
His byre, his bawn, and his threshing floor!
And oh, the swallows
Forget all wonders
When walls with the nests rise up once more."
   My strand is knit.

"Out of the dream
Of me, into
The round of his labor he will grow;
To spread his fields
In the winds of Spring,
And tramp the heavy glebe and sow;
And cut and clamp
And rear the turf
Until the season when they mow."
   My wheel runs smooth.

"And while he toils
In field and bog
He will be anxious in his mind—
About the thatch
Of barn and rick
Against the reiving autumn wind,
And how to make
His gap and gate
Secure against the thieving kind."
  My wool is fine.

"He has gone back;
No more I'll see
Mine image in his deepening eyes;
Then I'll lean above
The Well of the Bride,
And with my beauty, peace will rise!
O autumn star
In a hidden lake,
Fill up my heart and make me wise!"
  My quick brown wheel!

"The women bring
Their pitchers here
At the time when the stir of the house is o'er;
They'll see my face
In the well-water,
And they'll never lift their vessels more.
For each will say,
'How beautiful—

Why should I labor any more!
Indeed I come
Of a race so fair
'Twere waste to labor any more!' "
  My thread is spun.

II

(An older girl sings:)

One came before her and said beseeching,
"I have fortune and I have lands,
And if you will share in the goods of my house-hold
All my treasure's at your commands."

But she said to him, "The goods you proffer
Are far from my mind as the silk of the sea!
The arms of him, my young love, round me
Is all the treasure that's true for me!"

"Proud you are then, proud of your beauty,
But beauty's a flower will soon decay;
The fairest flowers they bloom in the Summer,
They bloom one summer and they fade away."

"My heart is sad, then, for the little flower
That must so wither where fair it grew—
He who has my heart in keeping,
I would he had my body too."

III

(An old woman sings:)

There was an oul' trooper went riding by
On the road to Carricknabauna,
And sorrow is better to sing than cry
On the way to Carricknabauna!
And as the oul' trooper went riding on
He heard this sung by a crone, a crone
On the road to Carricknabauna!

"I'd spread my cloak for you, young lad,
Were it only the breadth of a farthen',
And if your mind was as good as your word
In troth, it's you I'd rather!
In dread of any jealousy,
And before we go any farther,
Carry me up to the top of the hill
And show me Carricknabauna!"

"Carricknabauna, Carricknabauna,
Would you show me Carricknabauna?
I lost a horse at Cruckmoylinn—
At the Cross of Bunratty I dropped a limb—
But I left my youth on the crown of the hill
Over by Carricknabauna!"

Girls, young girls, the rush-light is done.
What will I do till my thread is spun?

SHE MOVED THROUGH THE FAIR

My young love said to me, "My brothers won't mind,
And my parents won't slight you for your lack of kind."
Then she stepped away from me, and this she did say,
"It will not be long, love, till our wedding day."

She stepped away from me and she moved through the fair,
And fondly I watched her go here and go there,
Then she went her way homeward with one star awake,
As the swan in the evening moves over the lake.

The people were saying no two were ere wed
But one had a sorrow that never was said,
And I smiled as she passed with her goods and her gear,
And that was the last that I saw of my dear.

I dreamt it last night that my young love came in,
So softly she entered, her feet made no din;
She came close beside me, and this she did say,
"It will not be long, love, till our wedding day."

I SHALL NOT DIE FOR THEE

O woman, shapely as the swan,
On your account I shall not die:
The men you've slain—a trivial clan—
Were less than I.

I ask me shall I die for these—
For blossom teeth and scarlet lips?
And shall that delicate swan shape
Bring me eclipse?

Well-shaped the breasts and smooth the skin,
The cheeks are fair, the tresses free—
And yet I shall not suffer death—
God over me!

Those even brows, that hair like gold,
Those languorous tones, that virgin way—
The flowing limbs, the rounded heel
Slight men betray!

Thy spirit keen through radiant mien,
Thy shining throat and smiling eye,
Thy little palm, thy side like foam—
I cannot die!

O woman, shapely as the swan,
In a cunning house hard-reared was I:
O bosom white, O well-shaped palm,
I shall not die!

OLD MEN COMPLAINING

FIRST OLD MAN:

He threw his crutched stick down: there came
Into his face the anger flame,
And he spoke viciously of one
Who thwarted him—his son's son.
He turned his head away. "I hate
Absurdity of language, prate
From growing fellows. We'd not stay
About the house the whole of a day
   When we were young,
Keeping no job and giving tongue!

"Not us in troth! We would not come
For bit or sup, but stay from home
If we gave answers, or we'd creep
Back to the house, and in we'd peep
Just like a corncrake.

"My grandson and his comrades take
A piece of coal from you, from me
A log, or sod of turf, maybe.
And in some empty place they'll light
A fire, and stay there all night,
A wisp of lads! Now understand
The blades of grass under my hand
Would be destroyed by company!

There's no good company! We go
With what is lowest to the low!
He stays up late, and how can he
Rise early? Sure he lags in bed
And she is worn to a thread
With calling him—his grandmother—
She's an old woman, and she must make
Stir when the birds are half awake
In dread he'd lose this job like the other!"

SECOND OLD MAN:

"They brought yon fellow over here,
And set him up for an overseer:
Though men from work are turned away,
That thick-necked fellow draws full pay,
Three pounds a week. . . . They let burn down
The timber yard behind the town
Where work was good, though firemen stand
In boots and brasses big and grand
The crow of a cock away from the place;
And with the yard they let burn too
The clock in the tower, the clock I knew
As well as I know the look of my face."

THIRD OLD MAN:

"The fellow you spoke of has broken his bounds—
He comes to skulk inside of these grounds:
Behind the bushes he lay down
And stretched full hours in the sun.

He rises now, and like a crane
He looks abroad. He's off again.
Three pounds a week, and still he owes
Money in every street he goes,
Hundreds of pounds where we'd not get
The second shilling of a debt."

"Old age has every impediment,
Vexation and discontent;
The rich have more than we: for bit
The cut of bread and over it
The scrape of hog's lard, and for sup
Warm water in a cup.
But different sorts of feeding breaks
The body more than fasting does
With pains and aches!

"I'm not too badly off, for I
Have pipe and tobacco, a place to lie,
A nook to myself; but from my hand
Is taken the strength to back command,
I'm broken, and there's gone from me
The privilege of authority."

I heard them speak—
The old men heavy on the sod,
Letting their angers come
Between them and the thought of God!

45

RIVER MATES

I'll be an otter, and I'll let you swim
A mate beside me; we will venture down
A deep, full river when the sky above
Is shut of the sun; spoilers are we:—
Thick-coated: no dog's tooth can bite at our veins,
With ears and eyes of poachers: deep-earthed ones
Turned hunters; let him strike past,—
The little vole; my teeth are on an edge
For the King-Fish of the River!
    I hold him up,
The glittering salmon that smells of the sea:
I hold him up and whistle!
    Now we go
Back to our earth: we will tear and eat
Sea-smelling salmon: you will tell the cubs
I am the Booty-bringer—I am the Lord
Of the River—the deep, dark, full, and flowing River.

DEDICATION
TO M. C. M. C.

The well—
They come to it and take
Their cup-full or their palms-full out of it.

The well—
Stones are around it, and an elder bush
Is there; a high rowan tree; and so
The well is marked.

Who knows
Whence come the waters? Through what passages
Beneath? From what high tors
Where forests are? Forests dripping rain!
Branches pouring to the ground; trunks, barks, roots,
Letting the streamlets down: through the dark earth
The water flows, and in that secret flood
That's called a spring, that finds this little hollow.
Who knows
Whence come the waters that fill cup and palm?

Sweetheart and comrade, I give you
The waters' marches and the forest's bound,
The valley-filling cloud, the trees that set
The rains beneath their roots, out of this well.

THE MONKEYS

Two little creatures
With faces the size of
A pair of pennies
Are clasping each other:
"Ah, do not leave me,"
One says to the other,
In the high monkey-
Cage in the beast-shop.

There are no people
To gape at them now,
For people are loth to
Peer in the dimness;
Have they not builded
Streets and playhouses,
Sky-signs and bars
To lose the loneliness
Shaking the hearts
Of the two little monkeys?

Yes. But who watches
The penny-small faces
Can hear the voices:
"Ah, do not leave me;
Suck I will give you,
Warmth and clasping,
And if you slip from

This beam, I can never
Find you again."

Dim is the evening,
And chill is the weather;
There, drawn from their colored
Hemisphere,
The apes liliputian
With faces the size of
A pair of pennies,
And voices as low as
The flow of my blood.

DUBLIN ROADS

When you were a lad that lacked a trade,
Oh, many's the thing you'd see on the way
From Kill-o'-the-Grange to Ballybrack,
And from Cabinteely down into Bray,
When you walked these roads the whole of a day.

High walls there would be to the left and right,
With ivies growing across their top,
And a briary ditch on the other side,
And a place where a quiet goat might crop,
And a wayside bench where a man could stop.

A hen that had found a thing in her sleep,
One would think, the way she went craw-craw-cree,
You would hear as you sat on the bench was there,
And a cock that thought he crew mightily,
And all the stir of the world would be

A cart that went creaking along the road,
And another cart that kept coming a-near;
A man breaking stones; for bits of the day
One stroke and another would come to you clear,
And then no more from that stone-breaker.

And his day went by as the clouds went by,
As hammer in hand he sat alone,
Breaking the mendings of the road;
The dazzles up from the stones were thrown,
When, after the rain, the sun down-shone.

And you'd leave him there, that stone-breaker,
And you'd wonder who came to see what was done
By him in a day, or a month, or a week:
He broke a stone and another one,
And you left him there and you travelled on.

A quiet road! You would get to know
The briars and stones along by the way;
A dozen times you'd see last year's nest;
A peacock's cry, a pigeon astray
Would be marks enough to set on a day;

Or the basket-carriers you would meet—
A man and a woman—they were a pair!
The women going beside his heel:
A straight-walking man with a streak of him bare,
And eyes that would give you a crafty stare.

Coming down from the hills they'd have ferns to sell,
Going up from the strand, they'd have cockles in stock:
Sand in their baskets from the sea,
Or clay that was stripped from a hillside rock—
A pair that had often stood in the dock!

Or a man that played on a tin-whistle:
He looked as he'd taken a scarecrow's rig;
Playing and playing as though his mind
Could do nothing else but go to a jig,
And no one around him, little or big.

And you'd meet no man else until you came
Where you could look down upon the sedge,
And watch the Dargle water flow,
And men smoke pipes on the bridge's ledge,
While a robin sang by the haws in a hedge.

Or no bird sang, and the bird-catchers
Would have talk enough for a battle gained,
When they came from the field and stood by the bridge,
Taking shelter beside it while it rained,
While the bird new-caught huddled and strained

In this cage or that, a linnet or finch,
And the points it had were declared and surmised:
And this one's tail was spread out, and there
Two little half-moons, the marks that were prized;
And you looked well on the bird assized!

Then men would go by with a rick of hay
Piled on a cart; with them you would be
Walking beside the piled-up load:
It would seem as it left the horses free,
They went with such stride and so heartily

And so you'd go back along the road.

FUCHSIA HEDGES IN CONNACHT

I think some saint of Eirinn wandering far
Found you and brought you here—
Demoiselles!—
For so I greet you in this alien air!

And like those maidens who were only known
In their own land as daughters of the King,
Children of Charlemagne—
You have, by following that pilgrim-saint
Become high votresses—
You have made your palace beauty dedicate,
And your pomp serviceable:
You stand beside our folds!

I think you came from some old Roman land—
Most alien, but most Catholic are you:
Your purple is the purple that enfolds
In Passion Week, the Shrine,
Your scarlet is the scarlet of the Wounds:
You bring before our walls, before our doors
Lamps of the Sanctuary;
And in this stony place
The time the robin sings,
Through your bells rings the Angelus!

AT THE FORE OF THE YEAR

At the fore of the year, and on Candlemas Day,
All early at Mass I remarked her—
Like the dew on green corn, as bright and as clear
Were her eyes, and her voice was the starling's!

With bragging and lies, I thought that her mind
I'd engage, and then win her with praises,
But through Spring and through Summer she has left me to rise
Every day with a pain that will slay me!

O come, O my love, ere the life from me goes
If your hand but to lightly lay on me,
And a grief take away that none else can remove—
For now 'tis the reaping of barley!

AT CASHEL

Above me stand, worn from their ancient use,
The King's, the Bishop's, and the Warrior's house,
Quiet as folds upon a grassy knoll:
Stark-grey they stand, wall joined to ancient wall,
Chapel, and Castle, and Cathedral.

It is not they are old, but stone by stone
Into another lifetime they have grown,
The life of memories an old man has:
They dream upon what things have come to pass,
And know that stones grow friendly with the grass.

The name has crumbled—CASHEL that has come
From conqueror-challenging CASTELLUM—
Walls in a name! No citadel is here,
Now as a fane the empty walls uprear
Where green and greener grass spreads far and near!

BLADES

Sojourner, set down
Your skimming wheel;
Nothing is sharp
That we have of steel:
Nothing has edge —
Oh, whirl around
Your wheel of stone
Till our blades be ground!

Harshly, quickly, under blades
Hafted with horn and wood and bone
Went the wheel:
Narrow long knives that should be one edge,
House-knives that sliced the loaf to the heel,
And scraped scales off mackerel,
And weighty knives that were shaped like a wedge —
Stone wakened keenness in their steel:
Knives with which besom-makers pare
Their heather-stalks, and hawkers' blades
Used by men of a dozen trades;
Broad-bladed knives that cut bacon-sides,
And stumpy knives for cobblers' hides,
With hunters' knives that were thinned with wear —
All were brought to,
All were laid on,
All were ground by
The Sojourner's wheel.

And those who filled the market-square
Saw hand and eye upon their ware
That were well-schooled and scrupulous
To spend upon that task their use.
But sparks came from the eyes and met
The sparks that were from edges whet,
As eagerly and wittingly
The dullness of each blade scoured he,
And the brow he bent was like a stone.

Over the grinding-stone he sang,
"The dalesman's sword shall make you fear,
And the dirk in the grasp of the mountaineer,
And likewise the pirate's blue cutlass
Who have left your blades long edgeless!"
But the men were thinking of games of cards,
And the looks of the boys were turned towards
The corner where they played pitch-and-toss
And the women thought of the herring across
The tongs to roast where pot-hooks hang.
"Unready and unforward men
Who have no right to any lien
On the gifts of Tubal Cain,
The gifts of our father, Tubal Cain!"

But no one drew meaning from the song,
As he made an equal edge along
One side of a blade and the other one,
And polished the surface till it shone.

"Now leave a blessing on what you have done."

"For what I have done I take my fee,
But no blessing I leave on it," said he,
"Everybody knows,
Everybody knows
That the knife-grinder
No blessing bestows."

Then the market-place, with wheel a-pack
He left, and the men to their cards went back
And talked of a bird in the cocker's loft;
.And of liming linnets beside the croft
And boys told between pitch and toss;
And the women laid the herring across
The tongs to roast for a sloven's meal.

And he went out beside the peel
Tower, and through Saint Selskar's Gate,
Heading at a hearty rate
Towards the hilltops and the shades.

And three who brought back sharpened blades
To their fathers' stalls by the Tan-yard Side,
And then stayed while a blackbird cried
Quietly by their groundsills —
The butcher's daughter,
The cobbler's daughter,
The hawker's daughter,
Were lost on the hills!

BRANDING THE FOALS

Why do I look for fire to brand these foals?
What do I need, when all within is fire?
And lo, she comes, carrying the lighted coals
And branding-tool—she who is my desire!
What need have I for what is in her hands,
If I lay hand upon a hide it brands,
And grass, and trees, and shadows, all are fire!

SCANDERBEG

She sat on the wall and dangled her silk-stockinged legs,
Saying, "I will not have them all stung for any old man who is
    dead,"
So I went where the nettles were rank and came on a stone that
    read,
"Matthew de Renzi,
Knight, born in Germany,
Descended from George Castriot, alias Scanderbeg,
Who fifty-two battles waged with conquest against the Great
    Turk."
More. the Knight de Renzi,
Learned in Irish, composed for it a Dictionary,
Corresponded with men of state upon affairs,
And died here; fifty-seven his years—
Peace be with Matthew!
Then I looked where she sat on the wall dangling her silk-
    stockened legs,
Which she would not have stung for any old man who was dead,
As she said—
Not even, I supposed, for a descendant of Scanderbeg!
But I heard a curlew
Over the river beside me, the Shannon it was,
And saw from that to the Danube, and it was crossed
By turbaned men under whose stallions' hooves the grass
Never grew again;
And that battlefield, the Plain of the Blackbirds, Kossovo,

And the Sultan Murad slain,

And the breach in Constantinople's wall, and Belgrade,

Buda and Vienna under great cannonade,

And the sweep of the Pashas onward till Hungary, Poland, the
Germanies were all dismayed,

And that historyless man, George Castriot, holding at bay

Byzantium's conquerors in the mountains of Albania;

Then battles along the Rhine,

And Dutchmen and English, Frenchmen and Irish, forcing or
holding this line,

And the Shannon crossed and Aughrim lost to our own over-
throw!

Two hundred years' battling in Europe at the name of Scanderbeg

Spun through my mind as a curlew cried overhead!

ASSES

"I know where I'd get
An ass that would do,
If I had the money—
A pound or two."

Said a ragged man
To my uncle one day;
He got the money
And went on his way.

And after that time
In market or fair
I'd look at the asses
That might be there.

And wonder what kind
Of an ass would do
For a ragged man
With a pound or two.

O the black and roan horses the street would fill,
Their manes and tails streaming, and they standing still,

And their owners, the men of estate, would be there,
Refusing gold guineas for a colt or a mare.

And one, maybe, riding up and down like a squire
So that buyers from Dublin might see and admire

The hunter or racer come to be sold.
And be willing and ready to pay out their gold.

With men slouching beside them and buyers not near
It's no wonder the asses held down head and ear.

They had been sold or in by-ways bought
For a few half-crowns tied up in a knot,

And no one so poor as to buy one might come
To that fair that had horses so well prized at home!

        And then it fell out
        That at Arva or Scrabbey,
        At some down-county fair,
        Or Mohill or Abbey,

        On two asses I happened—
        Without duress or dole
        They were there in the market,
        A dam and her foal.

        And the owner, a woman,
        Did not slouch or stand,
        But in her cart sitting
        Was as grand as the grand;

Like a queen out of Connacht
From her toe to her tip,
Like proud Grania Uaile
On the deck of her ship.

And her hair—'twas a mane:
The blackberries growing
Out of the hedge-rows
Have the sheen it was showing.

There kind was with kind
Like the flowers in the grasses
If the owner was fine,
As fine were her asses.

White, white was the mother
As a dusty white road;
Black on back and on shoulders
The cross-marking showed.

She was tall—she could carry
A youth stout of limb,
Or bear down from her mountain
The bride decked for him!

Such was the mother—
The foal's hide was brown,
All fleecy and curly,
And soft like bog-down;

And it nuzzled its mother,
Its head to her knee,
And blue were its eyes
Like the pools of the sea!

Then I thought all the silver
My uncle could draw
Might not pay for the creatures
That that day I saw;

And I thought that old Damer,
Who had troughs made of gold,
Could not pay for the asses,
The young and the old.

And I think of them still
When I see on the roads
Asses unyoked,
And asses with loads;

One running and trotting,
With harness loose,
And a man striking and hitting
Where his stick has use;

And one with a hide
Like a patched-on sack
And two creels of turf
Upon its back;

And one in the market,
Meek and brown,
Its head to the cart-shafts
That are down;

Eating its forage—
A wisp of hay;
In the dust of the highway
Munching away;

Unmarked in the market
As might be a mouse
Behind a low stool
In a quiet house—

Then I think of the pair
Horses might not surpass—
The dam and her foal,
The white ass and brown ass.

AN OLD SONG RE-SUNG

As I went down through Dublin city
At the hour of twelve of the night,
Who did I see but a Spanish lady
Washing her feet by candle light.
   First she washed them,
   Then she dried them,
   All by a fire of amber coals,
In all my life I never did see
A maid so neat about the soles.

I asked her would she come a-walking,
And we went on where the small bats flew,
A coach I called then to instate her,
And on we went till the grey cocks crew.
   Combs of amber
   In her hair were,
   And her eyes had every spell,
In all my life I never did see
A maid whom I could love so well.

But when I came to where I found her,
And set her down from the halted coach,
Who was there waiting, his arms folded,
But that fatal swordsman, Tiger Roache?
   Then blades were out,
   And 'twas thrust and cut,

And never wrist gave me more affright,
Till I lay low upon the floor
Where she stood holding the candle light.

But, O ye bucks of Dublin city,
If I should see at twelve of the night,
In any chamber, such lovely lady
Washing her feet by candle light,
   And drying o'er
   Soles neat as hers,
   All by a fire of amber coal —
Your blades be dimmed! I'd whisper her,
And take her for a midnight stroll!

CALL FOR THE BRIDE

For a bride you have come! Is it with a full score
Of rake-hell rapscallions you'd fill up my door,
With a drum to your tail and a fiddle before,
And a bag-piper playing all through ye?

My faith! Do you think that a shy little maid
Would lift up her head before such a brigade,
When an arm round her waist would make her afraid?
By my hand! She has gone from my keeping.

Through the gap in the hedges away she has run;
Like the partridge across the wide stubble she's gone,
And here I am, here I am, here I'm alone
With no daughter to give any comer!

Well, here she is back! I declare she has come
Like the cat to the cradle, and Nance she's at home:
O my love, would you go to the bleak hills of Crome,
Where nor manners nor mirth are in fashion?

O say not you'll go! That you'll never embark
From a plentiful house where you prize every spark,
Where there's milk in the crock and meal in the ark,
And a pair of fat ducks for the roasting!

Oh, mother sell all that you have to your name,
To give me a dowry to equal my fame—
Sell the cow, and the sow, and the gander that's lame,
And the sack of black wool in the corner!

And my good-will I'll leave to our Babe that stays here,
May she leave the bog-bottoms within the half-year,
Where the rushes are high and the curlews call near,
And the crows on the hills they are lonely.

With rake-hell young fellows my Babe will not go,
Nor look from her dormer on faction below,
From up where the picture and looking-glass show
That elegance holds and good order!

THE DEER OF IRELAND

An old man said, 'I saw
The chief of the things that are gone;
A stag with head held high,
A doe, and a fawn;

And they were the deer of Ireland
That scorned to breed within bound:
The last; they left no race
Tame on a pleasure-ground.

A stag, with his hide all rough
With the dew, and a doe and a fawn;
Nearby, on their track on the mountain,
I watched them, two and one,

Down to the Shannon going—
Did its waters cease to flow
When they passed, they that carried the swiftness
And the pride of long ago?

The last of the troop that had heard
Finn's and Oscar's cry;
A doe and a fawn, and before,
A stag with head held high!'

THE SPADESMAN

One man was still upon the ridge,
Spading potatoes from their clay;
The hareskin cap upon his head
Made him look wild—a man astray.

Creel-loads and pot-fulls he struck out—
Potatoes in the furrow thronged,
But still, as though the fading light,
The spended light, a spadesman wronged

He dug—the spade went down, and then,
Went down again; went down, went down;
The only sound came to us there,
His spade in clay, his spade on stone.

One said, 'These tenants were so racked,
With rent on field, on bog, on shore,
There was no reason but they saw
The bailiff's shadow on the door.

When others mustered to proclaim
With band and banner their leagued oath
To break the tenants' bondage, theirs—
How could this parish show its troth?

So poor they were—and this will show,
They had no share in parish band,
Neither a banner could they buy,
To give them name or prove their stand.

Then one bethought that blazing turfs
Set on pitchforks would do as well
As lettered banner with device,
Or fife-and-drum's uplifting swell.

And so they did, and I have heard
The ballad-singers praise the lads,
The pitchfork men who lifted up
The standard of the blazing sods.

I saw behind our man a line
Of parish folk, their pitchforks down,
Grasping the foregone spades to dig
A harvest that was all their own.

And there the man in hareskin cap
Toiling as though to lay with spade
The ghost of want, the ghost of blight
In the long furrow they had made.

But let that be! I single out
From folk of parish, odd and even
The man upon the ridge alone,
The man with spade, the man hard-driven.

AN OLD WOMAN SELLING DUCKS

They were hatched in the basket was under her bed,
And on her own floor
They were reared where she's seen them, between hob and threshold,
Between hearthstone and door!
And now to a market where prices are harried
Till they're nothing at all, the four ducks are carried!

And the time they's be gone her heart would be low,
And she'd murn an' murn,
And then they'd be back, and she'd hear in the lane
Their quack, quack of return;
And the cat would be vexed, and cross-eyed her looks
At the old body's joy when in came her ducks!

At noon they's be gone, but at dusk they'd be back
From the duck-pond in Urney,
And no hound would chase them that kept the good hours
On their back-and-forth journey;
No weasel nor wood-cat would near them and bite
An old body's ducks that were lucky and right!

From each end of the basket, too frightened to quack,
A duck sticks a beak,
And frightened is she, the old body who'd sell them,
And hardly will speak:
As she trudges along with her ducks, each as thin
As the water-hen!

CALEN O COSTURE ME

In Shakespeare's "Henry V" a song is mentioned by a first line which Professor
Gerard Murphy identifies as "Cailin o chois tSiuire me," meaning "I am a girl
from beside the Suir"—"a popular song in assonantal metre, otherwise lost."
The title gives rise to the idea of a girl from beside the Suir singing about herself
in Elizabethan London, and that idea is dramatized in this song:

I am a young girl
From beside the Suir,
Where like two shining harpstrings
Streams are clear and pure
Adown a slope of vendure
Where gorse has golden flower—
My thought must not be on them:
I look towards London Tower.

Would that there was beside me
Our wolfhound brave and great,
Who with a bound would shatter
The timber of yon gate,
And in the forecourt standing,
Would hold the guard at bay,
Until two captive Irishmen
Broke covert and away.

THE HEARTHSTONE AND THE LOOM

MAURICE

And we are here to look into a house
Where there's not even a forgotten stool,
You at the doorway, I where the window was.
I see the broken hearthstone.

TERENCE

      And I see
A patch of sunlight on the crumbled wall.
A loom was there; it was a young girl's own.

MAURICE

      Yes, where the window was.
And all around us are the places named
In legend while the pot boiled on the hearth—
Urney and Kevitt and Cullismore,
Famous for bluebells, nut-dells, an old rath,
Or ditches where the whins had brighter gold.

TERENCE

The clatter of the house gone with the smoke
Of peats new laid around the morning fire,
And burning rightly, brightly, quietly—
Clack of the loom was all the outer sound—

A beat, a measure of accord between
Her mind and loom, the shuttles and her hand.
It was a yard-long loom and framed for her
By an old uncle, a thoughtful man
Who kept in trim a dozen beds of flowers
Behind a fuschia hedge. My thread is weak
To cross to who he was or where he was,
But she sat there, young mistress of the loom
And wove the grey or brown and therewith dreamed
More glowing patterns in the days to be.

MAURICE

A change as great as any were foretold
In Columbkill's quaint prophecies is here—
Carriages without horses, and the hound
The calf displacing in the favored nook.
A broken quern-stone once held that gate:
A man from the Museum was searching for it,
But where it's gone there's nobody can tell.

TERENCE

This was the time when she was most herself:
She'd run to neighbours' houses, offer them
The things she wove, and brighter things than webs,
Things that she made with feathers and with flowers.
Like the wren's bevy ravelled from the nest,
Where no one knows they're gone.

MAURICE

But like the sun upon a patch of sail
Of vessel long delayed, the prophecy
Fulfilled, of the old stock restored,
And names contemned now honored to the full.

TERENCE

Now that her grand-daughter has come to wed
(She has the bright hair and the pointed face
That made the older kindred so remarked
By those who kept in mind the lineages)
She is bethought on. The time is when
The blackthorn's faint bloom is on the hedge.

MAURICE

What would you have fulfilled
For those who come into the after-story?

TERENCE

Bread eaten without debt to harden it,
Space in a house, no cark to waken to,
And no word said that brings an inner moan
And not a faithful answer; over these,
Work of the day that brings enough to keep
Brave an innocence in its walks and ways,
And festivals from time to time that mean
A share in revelry or in devotion,
And friends to take one out of the four walls
To some enjoyment that is like a ransom.

MAURICE

And so we turn from window-sill and door
Now that we only speak in prophecies.

THE BASKET-MAKER

A basket-maker, an itinerant,
His hands as supple as the rods he bended:
I stayed to buy the withied shape he made.

And then a friend
Who had the lore of ancient fields and houses
Came to me there (it was a market-place)

Four arm-rings of gold
In box of alder-bark was in his gleanings
Where the receding lake had left behind
A bronze-age village; a quern in its place
The grains it ground beside it—barley, wheat;
Two boar-tusk pendants and a piece of amber,
And under these, the woven hazel twigs
Laid down in summer, since the hazel nuts
Were not then filled; spindles and ox-yokes. . . .

I thought them apt, the woven hazel twigs
For there before us was a batch of them,
With rods that shone like amber-willow rods.
But my friend's mind was not engaged by them;
He left me with the man of supple hands—
Two of us only in the market-place.

No tool he had but his own hands, a knife
That he had used since his apprenticeship

Beside a pool
Where no one bided but the water-hen,
Or in a dell when hazel-nuts were green,
And the wren showed the bulky nest he made
To his small mate. I watched him weave
Rod over rod, no gaps between the ridges.
And thought upon 'the woven hazel twigs
Laid down in summer, since the hazel nuts
Were not then ripe.' I heard him say:
"The basket on the arm
Of the old woman out for marketing;
The wicker round
In which potatoes from the pot are poured;
The creel that brings the turf up from the bog;
The kish that holds them by the fireside:
There's no one marks them with a craftsman's name.
Scanted they are as commons of the house."

And there it is—my thought came back to me!
Your one that's known
At doors, as is the thatcher or the weaver,
Or by the din you make, as the horse-shoer,
Before your name gets into household speech.
For if you find and bring material
From willow-pool or hazel-dell far-off,
And make a thing that is of shape and use
Without bye-standers or the noise of tool,
You are not spoken of by men or women.
"The basket-maker has no name," he said.

But noteworthy! In Kerry glens, he told me,
Where grow the trees whose branches no one bends,
The old arbutus, the weavers' bundles
Are carried in his creels on asses' backs
Across the reeks; the silver ring he showed me,
With two hands clasped, a Claddagh granny gave him
For baskets were a benefit to carry
Her fish to Galway in. And there he ended
His discourse and his task: he got his shillings
And I the withied shape was to my liking.

I watched him go, his stock-in-trade upon him.
"I travel Ireland's length and breadth," he said.
There was dominion in the way he said it,
And in his even way towards other roofs,
A basket-maker, an itinerant.

THE BOOK OF KELLS

First, make a letter like a monument—
An upright like the fast-held hewn stone
Immovable, and half-rimming it
The strength of Behemoth his neck-bone,
And underneath that yoke, a staff, a rood
Of no less hardness than the cedar wood.
Then, on a page made golden as the crown

Of sainted man, a scripture you enscroll
Blackly, firmly, with the quickened skill
Lessoned by famous masters in our school,
And with an ink whose lustre will keep fresh
For fifty generations of our flesh.

And limn below it the Evangelist
In raddled coat, on bench abidingly,
Simple and bland: Matthew his name or Mark,
Or Luke or John; the book is by his knee,
And thereby its similitudes: Lion,
Or Calf, or Eagle, or Exalted Man.

The winds that blow around the world—the four
Winds in their colors on your pages join—
The Northern Wind—its blackness interpose;
The Southern Wind—its blueness gather in;
In redness and in greenness manifest
The splendours of the Winds of East and West.

And with these colors on a ground of gold
Compose a circuit will be seen by men
As endless patience, but is nether web
Of endless effort—a strict pattern:
Illumination lighting interlace
Of cirque and scroll, of panel and lattice.

A single line describes them and enfolds,
One line, one course where term there is none,
Which in its termlessness is envoying
The going forth and the return one.
With man and beast and bird and fish therein
Transformed to species that have never been.

With mouth a-gape or beak a-gape each stands
Initial to a verse of miracle,
Of mystery and of marvel (Depth of God!)
That Alpha or Omega may not spell,
Then, finished with these wonders and these signs,
Turn to the figure of your first outlines.

Axal, our angel, has sustained you so
In hand, in brain; now to him seal that thing
With figures many as the days of man,
And colors, like the fire's enamelling—
That baulk, that letter you have greatly reared
To stay the violence of the entering Word!

THE ARTIFICER

JAMES JOYCE

The long flight and asylum barely reached—
Asylum, but no refuge from afflictions
That bore on you and left you broken there—
This was the word was brought me: loneliness
That was small measure of the loneliness
That days and nights was with you, came to me.

Daedalus! Has your flight ended so?

I looked back to the days of our young manhood,
And saw you with the commons of the town
Crossing the bridge, and you
In odds of wearables, wittily worn,
A yachtsman's cap to veer you to the seagulls,
Our commons also, but your traffic
Sombre: to sell your books upon the quay.

And then, with shillings flushed,
To Barney Kiernan's for the frothy pints,
And talk that went with porter-drinkers there.
But you
Are also Schoolman, and these casual men
Are seen, are viewed by you in circumstance
Of history; their looks, their words
By you affirmed, will be looked back on,

Will be rehearsed. Nor they, nor I
Nor any other, will discern in you
The enterprise that you in secrecy
Had framed—to soar, to be the man with wings.

We did not know
The searching eyes beneath the peak of cap
Beheld
The Seventh City of Christendom
Re-famed. We did not know
Below your sayings there was incantation
To give the river back to twilight field,
River of discourse,
       Anna Livia,
River of fable,
       Plurabelle.

IN SAINT STEPHEN'S GREEN

Bare branches: on the tree above
A nest from seasons gone
That keeps in spite of all that blew
A lone, wild homeliness.

And they that have the lease of it,
Two magpies, flit around;
Their magpie-minds are bent upon
The matter of repair.

Renewal! Like some other beings,
They're claimant of a day
Whose grant is lodging, prospect, store,
Companionship renewed.

The magpies fly with tuft and twig
Up to the nest regained:
Elated by their enterprise
They patch, and probe, and pull.

And in the shadow, not a pair,
A triad: one lets fall
To one below the thread she's spun
Who measures, passes down

To one who's seated: on her lap
The shears, the cutting shears—
Three bronzen women at a task
That is from ancientry.

Like nuns of order so severe
None have remained but they:
They look out on a world where we
A homeliness repair.

EXPECTING NO ONE

The bridge we often crossed, one to the other—
I lean upon its ledge, expecting no one
From north or south, a pilgrim who is mindful
Of all he left behind, and mindful, too,
Of disrepair in all he has come back to.

The seagulls fly up from the darkened river—
Their flight disordered—there is emblem here.

I lean upon the ledge this stilly night—
The word that Thomas Moore has in his song
That's of departures—his statue is within
The watch I keep—the town's worst monument.
No more than he of "banquet hall deserted"
Am I in hope of one to re-appear.

Expecting no one—
Regretting this—that you had come so often
To where I crossed, and that so seldom I,
Moved from set purposes, made a festival
Of your approach, you who were attuned
To all the harps that sounded in the air.
And here I stand with all those purposes
Signed, sealed, delivered as a book in vault,
Between the statue in his metal cloak
And seagulls making their disordered flight,
Expecting no one from the south or north.

AFTER SPEAKING OF ONE WHO DIED
A LONG TIME BEFORE

"She should have had", I said, and then I stopped.
Knowing her want, how could I speak of it—
I who have only words of men befriended.
I should have had the language used by men
Who stood outside their tents, the waste before them,
And looking towards a great star made a poem
Of tenderness and grief, all manliness—
The words as lonely as their desert marches—
I should have had possession of that tongue
To make it known, the haplessness, the loss
Of one who went into a life forsaken.

And there were men in Ireland, annalists,
Unfailing men for whom all things had failed,
Whose chronicle was pillage would destroy
The vellum that they wrote on and make blank
A thousand years a people could take pride in,
And on a page that was the volume's end
Wrote of a personal loss, a wife or child
Dead, in words that have eventfulness
Being taken off the loom of history:
I should have had reversion of such words
To speak of all she lost in her life's decades.
"She should have had", you said, touched by what held me
"The simple things that we will always have".

DAY'S END

An old woman stands
By her house gable
Calling her chickens—
They run as they're able.

Leghorn, Dorking,
And Plymouth Rock:
They run where she holds
The open crock.

An old man, a poet,
On doorstep, although
No word's in his mouth
Is calling somehow

On words of deep meaning
That somewhere were said,
On faces like ballads
For street-singers made.

They run; they come to her,
The whole of her flock,
Counting the bantam
Hen and cock.

Evenings ten thousand
Were here and are gone,
Foxes that bear off
This one and that one.

"They're out", says the poet,
"Like the flame of the rush-
Candle; they're gone
Like a girl's first blush".

And the old woman's croon
Sounds lonely and far
Like voices that come
Where no footsteps are.

IRISH STUDIES
Richard Fallis, editor

Irish Studies presents a wide range of books interpreting important aspects of Irish life and culture to scholarly and general audiences. The richness and complexity of the Irish experience, past and present, deserves broad understanding and careful analysis. For this reason an important purpose of the series is to offer a forum to scholars interested in Ireland, its history, and culture. Irish literature is a special concern in the series, but works from the perspectives of the fine arts, history, and the social sciences are also welcome, as are studies which take multidisciplinary approaches.

Irish Studies is a continuing project of Syracuse University Press. Richard Fallis is associate professor of English at Syracuse University.

SELECTED POEMS OF PADRAIC COLUM

was composecd in 11 on 14 Baskerville on a Mergenthaler Linotron 202
by Eastern Graphics;
with display type in Folkwang;
printed by sheet-fed offset on 60-pound, acid-free Glatfelter Natural Hi-Bulk,
Smyth-sewn and bound over binder's boards in Holliston Roxite B,
with dust jackets printed in 2 colors
by Braun-Brumfield, Inc.;
designed by Mary Peterson Moore;
and published by

SYRACUSE UNIVERSITY PRESS
SYRACUSE, NEW YORK 13244-5160